Around the World
Clothing

Margaret C. Hall

Heinemann Library
Chicago, Illinois

Customer Service 888-454-2279

Visit our website at www.heinemannlibrary.com

Designed by Lisa Buckley
Printed in Hong Kong

05 04 03 02 01
10 9 8 7 6 5 4 3 2 1

Library of Congress Cataloging-in-Publication Data
Hall, Margaret, 1947-
     Clothing / Margaret C. Hall.
        p. cm. -- (Around the world)
     Includes bibliographical references and index.
     ISBN 1-58810-101-0 (library binding)
     1. Clothing and dress--Juvenile literature. [1. Clothing and dress.] I. Title. II. Around the world (Chicago, Ill.)

TT507 .H16 2001   391--dc21
                                                             00-063269

Acknowledgments
The author and publishers are grateful to the following for permission to reproduce copyright material:
Michael Scott/Tony Stone, pp. 1, 13; Wolfgang Kaehler, pp. 4a, 14,17, 20, 24; Keren Su/Tony Stone, pp. 4b, 9; Sharon Smith/Bruce Coleman, Inc., p. 4c; Kay Maeritz/Tony Stone, p. 5; BW Stitzer/Photo Edit, p. 6; John Shaw/ Bruce Coleman, Inc., p. 7; Glen Allison/Tony Stone, p. 8; David Hiser/Tony Stone, p. 10; Steve Lehman/Tony Stone, p. 11; JGG/Photo Edit, p. 12; Erica Lansher/Tony Stone, p. 15; Bill Avon/Photo Edit, p. 16; David Young-Wolff/Photo Edit, p. 18; Glen Allison/Tony Stone, p. 19; Wayne Eastep/Tony Stone, p. 21; Kim Saar/Heinemann Library, p. 22; Phil Martin/Heinemann Library, p. 23; Lawrence Migdale/Tony Stone, p. 25; Blaine Harrington III, p. 26; Terry Vine/Tony Stone, p. 27; D. MacDonald/Photo Edit, p. 28; Deborah Davis/Photo Edit, p. 29.

Cover: David Hiser/Tony Stone

Every effort has been made to contact copyright holders of any material reproduced in this book. Any omissions will be rectified in subsequent printings if notice is given to the publisher.

Some words are shown in bold, **like this.** You can find out what they mean by looking in the glossary.

Contents

People Have Needs

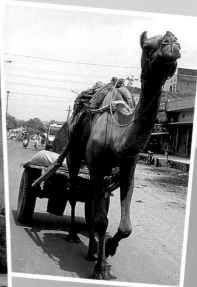

People everywhere have the same **needs.** They need food, clothing, water, and homes. They also need to be able to get from place to place.

Where people live makes a difference in what they eat and wear. It makes a difference in their homes and the kinds of **transportation** they use.

Why People Need Clothing

Clothing **protects** people from heat and cold. It helps them stay comfortable in different kinds of weather.

What a person wears sometimes tells something about him or her. It can tell about a person's **culture,** job, or **religious beliefs.**

Clothing Around the World

All around the world, many people wear
clothing that looks the same. However,
in some places, people wear clothing that
is very different.

What people wear depends on the **climate** where they live. It also depends on the **resources** they have close by.

Clothing for Cold Places

Some places get very cold. Winters are long, and it snows a lot. People need clothing that **protects** them from the cold.

When people go out in the cold, they
wear warm clothing. They cover as much
of their bodies as they can.

Cold-Weather Resources

Animals that live in cold **climates** have thick coats of **wool** or **fur.** These coats keep the animals warm.

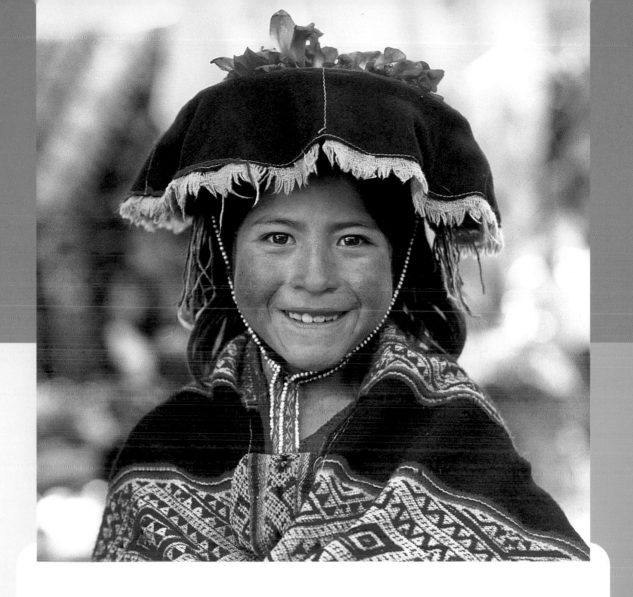

For thousands of years, people have used wool and fur from animals. They make it into clothing to keep themselves warm.

Clothing for Tropical Places

Some places have **tropical climates.**
The weather is very warm. Sometimes
there is a lot of rain.

People need special clothing to **protect** them from the hot sun. They also need clothing that will keep them dry when it rains.

Tropical-Weather Resources

In **tropical climates,** it is too warm to wear wool or fur. Instead, people use **fibers** from plants to make cloth for clothing.

Clothing made from plant fibers is lightweight. It is also cool and dries quickly when it gets wet.

Clothing for Desert Places

Deserts are very dry places. The days get very hot, but nights are cool. High winds can blow sand all around.

People who live in deserts wear clothing that **protects** them from blowing sand. Their clothing keeps them cool when it is hot and warm when it is cool.

Desert Resources

People in **desert** countries wear clothing made from **cotton** or **wool.** Cotton is used for cool clothing. Wool is used for warmer clothing.

People wear robes and head coverings to **protect** them from the hot sun. Loose clothing lets the air cool off the body, too.

Clothing for Safety

People who do dangerous jobs need special clothing to keep them safe. Firefighters need hats, coats, and boots that can **protect** them from fire and smoke.

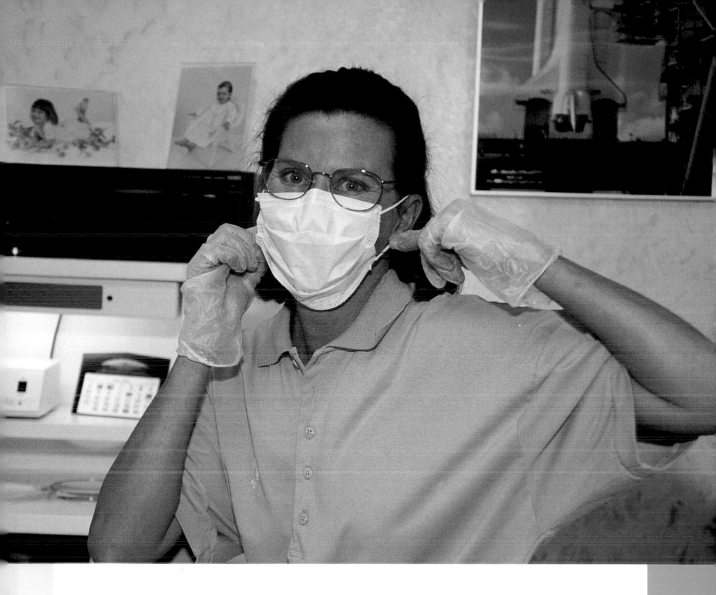

Some workers wear special clothing to keep things clean or to keep **germs** from spreading. That is why a doctor wears a mask and gloves.

Clothing for Work

Some people wear special clothes that tell others what their job is. Nurses, soldiers, and mail carriers wear **uniforms.**

People who wear uniforms for outside jobs have to be **protected** from the weather. They may have different uniforms for hot and cold weather.

City Clothing

In large cities around the world, people dress a lot alike. Office workers often wear suits or dresses.

Most buildings in large cities are heated in the winter and air-conditioned in the summer. People don't need special clothing when they are inside.

Special Clothing

Some people wear special clothing because of their **religious beliefs.** Some men may cover their heads or grow beards. Women may cover their faces or wear skirts instead of pants.

In some **cultures,** people wear **traditional** clothing for special days. This clothing often looks like what people of that culture wore long ago.

Amazing Clothing Facts

✪ A child of Samoa may wear a piece of cloth wrapped around the waist called a "lava lava." It can be worn as a skirt, a dress, a bathing suit, or pajamas!

✪ The first cloth ever made was probably linen. It is made from **fibers** of the flax plant, which grows best in cool, rainy places. Linen is still used to make clothing today.

✪ If you looked at **wool** fibers under a microscope, you would be surprised. The fibers are covered with **scales** that help to shed water. That is one reason why wool makes warm winter clothing.

✪ Today a lot of clothing is made from oil and natural gas. Polyester, rayon, and dacron are just a few kinds of cloth made from fibers invented by scientists.

Glossary

climate   year-to-year weather for an area

cotton   plant with fluffy white balls of fiber that are used to make lightweight cloth

culture   beliefs and practices of a group of people

desert   place with a very dry climate

fiber   thread-like part of a plant used to make cloth

fur   hairy coat of some animals

germ   tiny living organism that spreads disease

needs   things people must have in order to live

protect   to keep safe

religious beliefs   what a person believes about God

resource   item available for use

scale   small, thin plate that forms a covering

traditional   way something has been done or made for a long time

transportation   ways people move from place to place

tropical   place where the weather is hot and rainy

uniform   clothing that tells the job of the person who is wearing it

wool   soft, wavy hair of some animals that can be made into cloth

More Books to Read

Ajmera, Maya, and Anna Rhesa Versola. *Children from Australia to Zimbabwe*. Watertown, Mass.: Charlesbridge, 1997. An older reader can help you with this book.

Bryant-Mole, Karen. *Clothes*. Chicago, Ill.: Heinemann Library, 1998.

Jackson, Mike. *Clothing from Many Lands*. Austin, Tex.: Raintree Steck-Vaughn Company, 1995.

Index